cool science

Wireless Technology

Mary Firestone

LERNER PUBLICATIONS COMPANY
MINNEAPOLIS

This book is dedicated to
my brothers, Robin and
Michael Berger

Lerner Publications Company
A division of Lerner Publishing Group, Inc.
241 First Avenue North
Minneapolis, MN 55401 U.S.A.

Website address: www.lernerbooks.com

Library of Congress Cataloging-in-Publication Data

Firestone, Mary.
      Wireless technology / by Mary Firestone.
          p.   cm. — (Cool science)
      Includes bibliographical references and index.
      ISBN 978-0-8225-7590-0 (lib. bdg. : alk. paper)
      1. Wireless communication systems—Juvenile literature. I. Title.
    TK5103.2.F525 2009
    621.384—dc22   2007041102

Manufactured in the United States of America
1 2 3 4 5 6 – BP – 14 13 12 11 10 09

Table of Contents

Introduction

It's a beautiful day in the park, and you're enjoying the sunshine and the company of your friends. Then you remember. You have to do research for your science project. Hey, no problem. Your laptop is right next to you. There in the grass, you begin searching the Internet for ideas as birds chirp in the background.

Laptop computers make it easy to take the Internet everywhere.

Wireless technology puts information at your fingertips from practically anywhere in the world. It allows you to connect with friends, family, and others with ease—even if there isn't a telephone line for miles around. Wireless technology sets you free, so you can create a workspace (or fun space) from practically anywhere.

Modern technology has given us easy, convenient ways to transfer information, communicate, and entertain ourselves. With wireless technology, we can do all these things on devices that work without wires or cables. Wireless technology includes cell phones, wireless Internet connections, and handheld devices such as PDAs. Medical devices such as cardiac pacemakers rely on wireless technology to correct heart rhythms. A Global Positioning System (GPS) uses satellites and wireless technology to help people know where on Earth they are and how to get where they're going.

Not long ago, if you wanted privacy for a phone call, you needed a long cord to pull the phone into another room. If you wanted to surf the Internet, you had to do it in your home, your office, or on a public computer at the library. Not too long ago, you had to stand up and turn a knob on the TV to change the channel.

That's all changed. In modern times, you can chat with friends on a wireless Bluetooth headset, send e-mails on your BlackBerry, and download a new song to your iPod. And you can do it all without leaving that sunny spot in the park.

chapter 1

What Is Wireless Technology?

Wireless technology lets you send and receive information without using wires. It can be said to include simpler, older devices like car radios and baby monitors—even garage door openers and TV remotes. But when we talk about wireless technology, we mean electronic devices that are linked, or networked, together. These devices can send and receive large amounts of information over radio waves.

Radio Waves

Radio waves are energy waves that move through space at a certain frequency (or wavelength). Other kinds of waves travel the same way. These include microwaves, visible light, and X-rays. Different kinds of waves travel at different frequencies. A wave's frequency is how often it goes up and down in one second.

X-rays have a different wavelength than visible light.

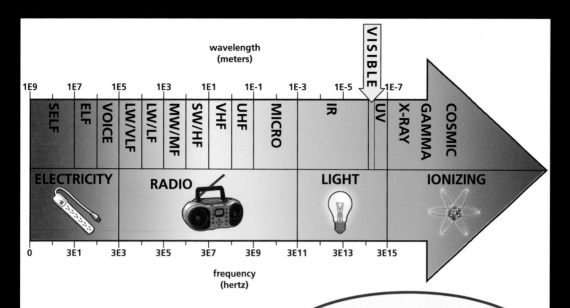

wavelength (meters)

| 1E9 | 1E7 | 1E5 | 1E3 | 1E1 | 1E-1 | 1E-3 | 1E-5 | 1E-7 |

VISIBLE

| SELF | ELF | VOICE | LW/VLF | LW/LF | MW/MF | SW/HF | VHF | UHF | MICRO | IR | UV | X-RAY | GAMMA | COSMIC |

ELECTRICITY   **RADIO**   **LIGHT**   **IONIZING**

| 0 | 3E1 | 3E3 | 3E5 | 3E7 | 3E9 | 3E11 | 3E13 | 3E15 |

frequency (hertz)

This diagram shows the electromagnetic spectrum. Radio waves have a lower frequency and longer wavelength than visible light.

Nearly any information can be transmitted wirelessly, including sounds, text, images, and video. To do this, you need three basic parts:

1. a transmitter
2. a receiver
3. a carrier wave

The transmitter and receiver are electronic devices. They use wires and hardware to function. The carrier wave begins as a continuous wave pattern. But to carry information, it has to be modulated, or changed.

IT'S A FACT!

Radio stations broadcast news and music on radio waves. Your radio receives the waves, so you can hear the broadcasts. Radio waves are one kind of electromagnetic wave, which are all around us. Everything in the universe gives off electromagnetic waves, even you.

For example, the sounds in a telephone conversation produce movements called vibrations. These are combined in the transmitter with a constant radio wave, or carrier wave. When they're combined, the radio wave has been modulated. The two signals travel together through the air. Modulation changes information on the wave into codes a receiver can understand.

Wi-Fi routers, antennas, and cell phone towers are transmitters. They modulate sounds and images over radio waves. Computers, cell phones, and other devices are the receivers.

Radio transmitter towers (left) strengthen and broadcast radio waves carrying sound signals. Individual radios (above) receive the waves and translate them back into sound vibrations.

History of Wireless Communication

Electromagnetic waves were first described by a physicist named James Clerk Maxwell. He published a paper in 1864 explaining how light waves and radio waves move through space. At the time, people could communicate by electrical telegraph. Telegraphs send messages over wires, using Morse code. A practical telephone wasn't invented until 1876.

Maxwell's theory was proven by physicist Heinrich Hertz. In the 1880s, Hertz did experiments with a simple transmitter and receiver set apart from each other. When the transmitter produced a spark, the receiver responded with a smaller spark. This experiment showed that electrical energy had traveled across the room, wirelessly.

The Electrical Telegraph and Morse Code

Samuel Morse and Alfred Vail created Morse code in the 1840s. The code is a series of dots and dashes that correspond with letters of the alphabet. The dots and dashes were sent over cables by using a tapping device on an electric telegraph. Blinking lights from shore were also used to send messages in Morse code from land to ships.

The U.S. Navy used another method. Sailors stood on decks of ships holding flags in different positions that symbolized letters of the alphabet.

A British sailor signals another boat using flags. The flags are divided diagonally into two colors, usually red and yellow. This system is known as semaphore.

Guglielmo Marconi

A young Italian inventor named Guglielmo Marconi read about Maxwell and the experiments of Hertz. He then took wireless technology a step further. He created a wireless telegraph that could send a message without wires. Other scientists had created similar devices, but Marconi's wireless telegraph was the most reliable. It could also send messages over long distances. Like Hertz, Marconi used a transmitter and a receiver.

On May 13, 1897, Marconi sent the first wireless message over water. He sent a message 8.7 miles (14 kilometers) over the Bristol Channel in Great Britain. The message was "Are you ready?" In December 1901, Marconi's equipment transmitted the first message to cross an ocean, a Morse code letter *S*. The message traveled from Cornwall, England, across the Atlantic to Saint John's, Canada, just over 2,100 miles (3,500 km). He'd proved that wireless signals could travel over thousands of miles.

Guglielmo Marconi operates an early model of his wireless telegraph machine.

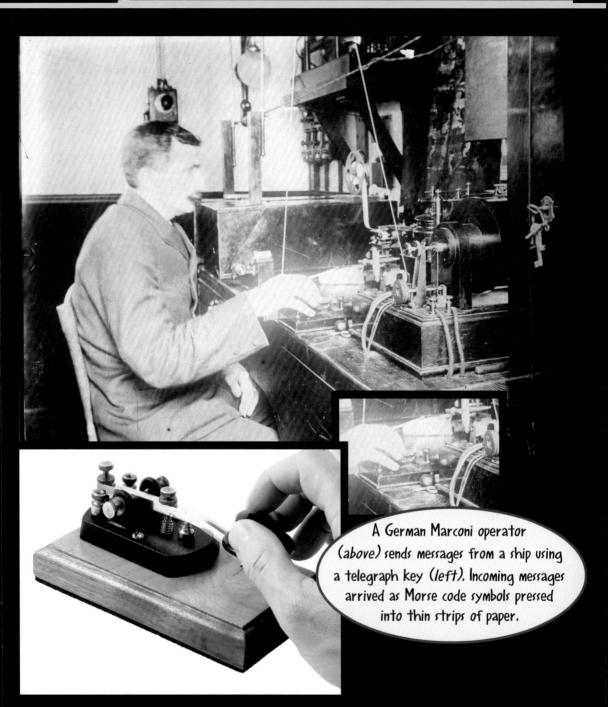

A German Marconi operator (*above*) sends messages from a ship using a telegraph key (*left*). Incoming messages arrived as Morse code symbols pressed into thin strips of paper.

Ships were soon using Marconi's equipment to communicate with ports. By 1907 all transatlantic ocean liners carried Marconi Company radio equipment. His specially trained telegraph operators tapped out news or sent requests for help if the ships were in trouble.

The Marconi and the *Titanic*

The *Titanic*, a spectacular luxury ocean liner, struck an iceberg in the dark of night in 1912. It sank to the floor of the Atlantic, killing more than fifteen hundred people. However, seven hundred were saved. Marconi's telegraph operators were able to reach neighboring vessels with distress signals. It later became law that all large ships must carry wireless systems.

This illustration shows what people might have seen while escaping from the sinking Titanic.

Advances in Wireless Technology

With Marconi's work, the world began to seem smaller. Wireless technology made it possible for people all over the world to communicate. New advancements quickly followed. In 1919 the first radio show was broadcast just for entertainment. Radio pioneer Lee De Forest invented a unique vacuum tube that strengthened weak audio signals. He was also the first to broadcast commercials over radio.

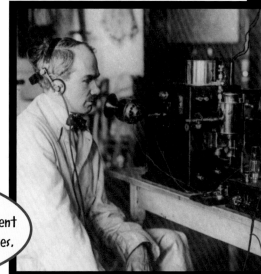

Lee De Forest (*right*) was one of the first people to play music for entertainment on the radio. He broadcast opera performances.

Color television was invented in 1940. But until the late 1960s, most people did not have color televisions to receive broadcasts in color.

Wireless technology has improved steadily over the years. Television images were transmitted wirelessly during the 1920s. After World War II (1939–1945), sales of television sets grew wildly. In 1957 the world's first artificial, or human-made, satellite was launched into space. It transmitted a radio signal that was received on Earth. The United States launched *Echo I* in 1960. It was the first communications satellite. Microwaves were sent into space, and *Echo I* bounced them back to another location on Earth. This system was used by the U.S. government to transmit telephone calls across continents.

In the 1960s, the U.S. government began developing the Internet. This network of computers communicates electronically. It was not wireless yet, but it set the stage for big changes in wireless technology.

chapter 2

Computer Unchained

In the 1980s, personal computers (PCs) became common. Many public places such as libraries and universities had them. So did many people's homes. Information was stored on hard drives and floppy disks. By the late 1990s, most personal computers were also hooked up to the Internet. This allowed computers to exchange information electronically through e-mail and the World Wide Web.

Early personal computers were large and expensive.

The Internet totally changed the way we communicate. We can transmit and receive text, images, sound, and video with a simple mouse click. We can chat with friends electronically, play games with players all over the world, and do research, all from a PC. For many young people, it's impossible to imagine a world without the Internet.

In the late 1980s, companies began developing computers and components that could network, or communicate, wirelessly. But each company's products could network only with other products made by the same company. People were used to combining electronic products from different companies—a video player made by one company and a TV set by another, for example. Wireless networking didn't get popular for that reason.

Networks

If you use a wireless network in your home or school, it is probably a WLAN, or wireless local area network. WLANs cover a small area, like a home, library, office, or school. Other types of networks include:

Campus Area Networks (CANs) are made up of connected LANs to make a larger area network.

Metropolitan (or Municipal) Area Networks (MANs) are large enough to encompass a city.

Personal Area Networks (PANs) are limited to a few feet around one person.

All these networks can be wireless or not.

Eventually, electronics companies agreed they needed a wireless standard—a single technology that all wireless computer products could use. A committee was formed to create that standard. Committee members represented several companies. In 1997 the committee introduced Wi-Fi to the public. "Wi-Fi" is short for "wireless fidelity."

Aquest parc està equipat amb accés a Internet sense fils.
Per connectar des del seu dispositiu WiFi, seleccioni la xarxa HOTSPOT (max. 2 hores)

This park is equiped with access to the Internet throught a wireless lan.
To connect your WiFi device select the HOTSPOT lan (max. 2 hours)

This sign tells Internet users in a park how to connect to the local Wi-Fi network.

A router (above) broadcasts the Wi-Fi signal. Computers use a wireless network card (below) to receive and translate the signals.

In July 1999, Apple Computer, Inc., released the first Wi-Fi–compatible computer, the iBook. Other computer makers quickly followed. People no longer had to connect their computers to phone lines or cables to access the Internet. They could surf the Web on wireless computers.

Wi-Fi starts with a wired Internet connection and a router. The router receives information over cables hooked up to the Internet and translates it into a modulated radio signal. It then transmits the radio waves for computers or other devices in the area to receive.

With a laptop and a wireless connection, you can jump on the Internet anywhere there's a Wi-Fi network. Wireless networks are in many libraries, cafés, restaurants, airports, and people's homes. Even entire cities are becoming wireless hotspots, providing free or inexpensive wireless access to people who live there. Wireless networks are becoming so common that it won't be long before you can access the Internet wirelessly from just about anywhere.

IT'S A FACT!

In 2004 a surfboard designer in Great Britain designed a board with a PC built in. The PC was equipped with Wi-Fi and a webcam. The webcam recorded the surfer's surroundings, and the computer streamed the video to the Internet. This allowed Web surfers to see the waves close-up, just like the real surfer.

Using Intel's Wi-Fi surfboard, pro surfer Duncan Scott can keep track of tides, check e-mail, and get weather reports.

Wireless Frequency Bands for Wireless Communication

Radio waves can be broadcast at different frequencies. Governments assign specific frequency bands to be used for specific purposes. This helps keep the radio waves from interfering with one another. In the United States, the Federal Communications Commission (FCC) decides which radio frequencies can be used for which purposes.

Wi-Fi in the United States transmits at 2.4 GHz or 5 GHz. "GHz" is an abbreviation of "gigahertz." That means one billion cycles per second. A Wi-Fi radio wave bounces up and down 2.4 billion times per second or 5 billion times per second, depending on which frequency it uses.

Cellular systems operate in the 824 MHz to 894 MHz radio frequency bands. "MHz" stands for "megahertz" and means one million cycles per second. You can see that cellular phones operate at a much lower frequency than Wi-Fi. That's because higher frequencies can carry more data. Wi-Fi needs the higher frequency to carry all the information that is transmitted on the Internet.

Most remote control cars operate at 27 or 49 megahertz. Running two cars on the same frequency can confuse the signals and cause crashes.

Anything that uses radio waves has to use a certain frequency. That includes garage door openers, cordless phones, remote control toys, AM and FM radio stations—and even air traffic control communication.

This Wi-Fi base station has been mounted on a streetlight. The network provides Wi-Fi to an entire city.

The 2.4 GHz and 5 GHz frequencies used for Wi-Fi are unlicensed. That means they are set up for public access. Individuals, companies, and cities can make their own hotspots in this range without being licensed. (Radio stations, television stations, and other users of radio waves have to be licensed.)

Wireless Security Alert

Most public wireless hotspots, like those in coffee shops and libraries, are open networks. That means they're available to everyone. But open networks aren't password protected. Tech-savvy snoopers can get on them and see what users are doing. They can steal credit card information, attach viruses that can damage your computer, and even read your e-mail.

Wireless users can protect themselves against snoopers by protecting passwords and installing security programs.

This doesn't have to stop you from enjoying Wi-Fi, though. There's plenty of good (and often free) software available to protect your privacy. If you have a home network, make sure it is password protected.

WiMAX

As the demand for wireless service grows, technology has grown right along with it. The recent upgrade in wireless is WiMAX.

One drawback of Wi-Fi is that it is not always as fast as broadband access (high-speed wired Internet). Another problem is that hotspots are usually small and not always available. As you move around, you might move out of the hotspot's range. Even if you stay connected, your connection slows the farther you move away from the router.

Motorola released this WiMAX gateway device in 2008. A gateway creates a small WiMAX network, while towers create large networks.

WiMAX, or worldwide interoperability for microwave access, will solve these problems. WiMAX is expected to be in common use soon. Like Wi-Fi, it will provide wireless Internet access—but at a much higher speed. And unlike Wi-Fi, WiMAX is a mobile Internet technology. Its signal is broadcast from big towers just as cellular phone signals are. That means it can hand off a signal from antenna to antenna, as cell phones do. You never lose your connection.

Experts say in the near future, most of our handheld, laptop, and home computers will be equipped with both Wi-Fi and WiMAX.

IT'S A FACT!
A WiMAX tower can provide coverage to a huge area—up to 3,000 square miles (about 8,000 sq. km).

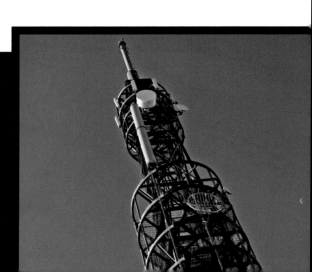

chapter 3

Cell Phones and PDAs

The beauty of wireless technology is that it gives you freedom. Few devices offer as much freedom as cellular phones and PDAs.

> Cell users can personalize their phones with different colors and patterns.

Cellular phones (also called mobile phones or cell phones) are the most well-known wireless devices. Cell phones don't need phone lines or phone jacks. You can carry them with you and make phone calls from almost anywhere. Cell phones equipped with a GPS can help you locate where you are. Cell phones even play an important role as a safety device.

Towers and Cells

Like Wi-Fi, cell phone connections are made with radio waves. But cell phone signals are different from Wi-Fi signals. Cell phone signals are broadcast on much lower frequencies and can carry only voices, not data.

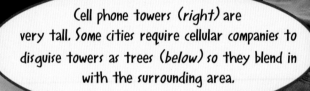

Cell phone towers (right) are very tall. Some cities require cellular companies to disguise towers as trees (below) so they blend in with the surrounding area.

A Wi-Fi hotspot usually has a small range. But cell phone signals can be broadcast over wide areas. Each broadcast area is called a "cell." That's how cell phones got their name. Each cell has a building containing radio equipment and a tall tower. The tower broadcasts the signals. Callers can stay connected to a single phone call even if they travel outside of a tower's cell. That's because cellular towers hand the signal off from cell to cell.

When you turn on your cell phone, it takes a moment to locate the control channel frequency. That's the frequency the phone and base station use to talk to each other. When your cell phone is fully charged and connected, you can make a call.

Cell phones are duplex devices. This means they use two radio frequencies at the same time. One transmits sound, and one receives it. This enables two people to talk at the same time. Compare this to walkie-talkies and CB radios. These simplex devices use only one frequency. They allow only one speaker to talk at a time.

Cell phone technology was developed in the 1980s. But it wasn't until the early 1990s that cell phones really became common. That's when cell phones became digital. Digital cell phones could connect faster and send clearer signals. They were more affordable, and they were built small enough to comfortably carry anywhere.

Modern cell phones do much more than make calls. They are equipped with games, calendars, and GPS. These phones have microphones and video cameras. You can also send a text message on your cell phone.

The Motorola Talkabout T900 sends text messages and receives e-mail wirelessly.

IT'S A FACT!

Cell phone texting even has its own language of abbreviated terms such as *BRB* (be right back), *GTG* (got to go), *LOL* (laugh out loud), and *IDK* (I don't know).

In 1996 cell phones began to change again. A new technology was developed that allowed cell phones to access the Internet. By the early 2000s, a new generation of cell phones, called smartphones, was common. Users could check e-mail and browse the Web with special applications made for the small screen of a cell phone.

Smartphones are really phones combined with small personal computers. The most well-known of these is the iPhone. Smartphones have all the cool stuff regular cell phones have and more. They have touch screens and full keyboards. They have word-processing programs, PDF viewers, Web browsers with Wi-Fi, and e-mail. If you want to watch news, sports, or TV clips, you can do that too. You can even watch a movie on some smartphones.

In addition to the iPhone, new smartphones include the Helio Ocean, Motorola RIZR, and BlackBerry Pearl 8100.

Face Dialing

Touch-screen technology on the iPhone is sensitive. In fact, its engineers worried that people's faces might press buttons during calls. This could disconnect calls, call other people, or even start programs like Web browsers. "Face dialing" could be a big problem! To prevent this, the engineers installed sensors that switch the touch screen off when the phone gets close to your ear. This prevents you from accidentally hitting any buttons. It also preserves battery life. The screen pops back on when the phone moves away from your face.

The Apple iPhone also has an MP3 player.

PDAs (Personal Digital Assistant)

Closely related to smartphones are personal digital assistants, or PDAs. The term *PDA* was coined by John Sculley in 1992, when he was chief executive officer of Apple. The original PDA was a portable electronic organizer that could share information with a PC. It was meant to be an extension of the home computer, not a replacement.

PDAs took off in the late 1990s when, like cell phones, they gained Internet and e-mail access. Modern PDAs are portable, wireless computers. Besides Internet access, they have word processing, spreadsheets, calendars, address books, and GPS. They can play music, scan bar codes, and record video. Computers used to be as big as refrigerators. But you can carry a PDA in your pocket.

PDAs like the BlackBerry and Treo offer small keyboards and thumb-wheels, making it easier to surf the Web. You can also plug in a full-size keyboard. This is helpful if a project requires a lot of writing. A tiny keyboard is handy for brief notes and e-mails, but you wouldn't want to write long letters or reports that way.

The BlackBerry *(left)* lets users read e-mail, schedule meetings, and take notes on their cell phones. About eight million people were using BlackBerry phones in 2007.

Say you're at a friend's house. You download a great song onto your PDA using his Wi-Fi connection. Later, you want to listen to it on your stereo at home. Do you have to connect your PDA to your computer with wires, upload the song to your computer, and then burn a disc to play in your CD player?

No way, not when there's Bluetooth. With Bluetooth you simply send the song from your PDA to your stereo—wirelessly.

Logitech released a wireless keyboard and mouse *(below)* in 2003. In 2007 Oakley invented stereo eyewear *(left)*. These sunglasses include a cell phone headset and a music player.

King Bluetooth

The name Bluetooth refers to King Harald I, a famous Danish king of the tenth century. His nickname was Bluetooth. He united the nations of Scandinavia after they'd been torn apart by wars and feuding. The founders of Bluetooth SIG (a special interest group of computer industry leaders) picked the name because the standard was first developed in Scandinavia. Like King Harald uniting Scandinavian nations, Bluetooth unites differing technologies and industries.

Sources vary on why King Harald Blaatand got the name Bluetooth. Some say he loved blueberries, which he ate in such large quantities that they stained his teeth. Others say that one of his teeth was darkened.

So what is Bluetooth? It's a short-range wireless standard that allows you to connect many different devices, easily and simply, without wires. Bluetooth replaces the wires that run between devices, like a PDA and a stereo. It's also used to replace the wires between your mouse and keyboard, and your keyboard and computer.

Imagine a home that has a stereo system, a TV, and a DVD player. Imagine it also has a cordless phone, a cellular phone, a PDA, and a laptop computer. If each of these systems has Bluetooth, they can form their own network, called a piconet. A piconet is controlled by one master device (such as a computer or PDA) that talks to up to seven "slave" devices.

Amazon.com's Kindle reading device uses the same network as cell phones. Users do not need to be near a Wi-Fi hotspot to download books and newspapers.

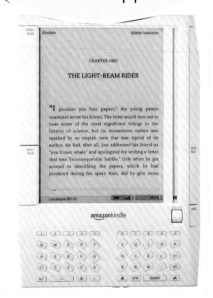

Piconets have many uses. These robots are part of a piconet experiment on a Bluetooth network. The laptop tells the robots where to go, and the robots send information about the location back to the computer. Someday, groups of piconet robots could be used to get information about places where humans cannot go.

In a piconet, all the devices can talk to one another about volume, program selections, e-mail alerts, and more. For example, the TV can inform you if you have a text message on your cell phone. Your cell phone can let you know you have an e-mail on your computer.

Best of all, the devices form this piconet without a user having to do anything. They know how to connect, and they do it themselves.

Bluetooth software comes standard on many wireless systems, including PDAs, cell phones—and even headsets. Enjoy that song you just downloaded in yet another way. Send it from your PDA to your Bluetooth-enabled headphones. You can stroll around your home listening to it, completely free of wires.

Chapter 4

Satellite
Communications

Have you ever ridden in a car that gives the driver directions? A device on the dashboard shows a map, and a voice tells the driver when to turn and how far to go. You never have to worry about getting lost, because the device always knows exactly where you are. Devices like this get their information from GPS satellites.

GPS devices can be part of the car, or users can buy them separately. This driver's PDA includes a GPS device.

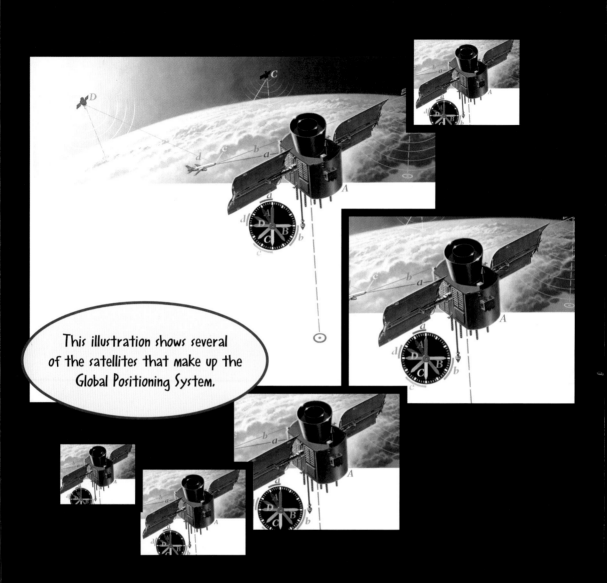

This illustration shows several of the satellites that make up the Global Positioning System.

Global Positioning System

The Global Positioning System is made up of twenty-four satellites. The satellites orbit—and transmit signals to—Earth. GPS devices receive the signals and figure out your exact location. They can also tell you other things, such as how fast you're going. They can tell you how far you've gone in a given time and how far you have to go to get to your destination. GPS devices can give you directions and even tell you the exact time the Sun will set or rise where you are.

The futuristic Aptera Type-1 car includes a GPS unit in the dashboard. The car can run on electicity or on a combination of electricity and gas.

GPS devices have lots of uses. They can save the lives of lost mountain climbers and help travelers find their way around a new city. They can calm parents' nerves when their teenagers start driving. A small device in the car relays the car's location and speed of travel to a website. If the speed is higher than it should be, Mom and Dad get a cell phone alert. Caught!

If you're a skier or snowboarder who enjoys skiing off the trails, you should let others know where you are. A new handset called the SPOT Satellite Messenger can do that by using a satellite phone network. It transmits your location to cell phones you've selected. It has an SOS button too. It will automatically dial 911 when you punch it.

GPS can also enhance workouts and make traveling more fun. Runners, hikers, rafters, and cross-country skiers can use GPS devices to plan their routes and track their progress. Even more fun, athletes and travelers can join social networking websites where members can track other members of their community in real time using Google Maps. Members can upload photos, video, or text to specific map locations to share what they experienced on their trip.

GPS is used in all forms of transportation. Meteorologists use GPS to forecast and study the weather. Geologists use it for studying earthquakes. GPS can even help you track a lost dog. A gadget attached to the dog's collar transmits its location to a device you carry in your hand.

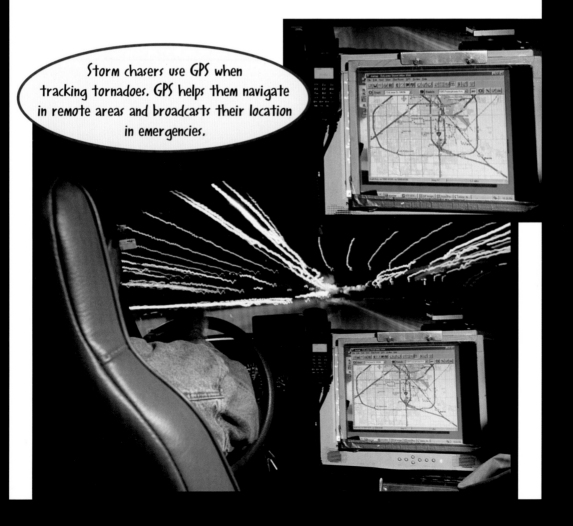

Storm chasers use GPS when tracking tornadoes. GPS helps them navigate in remote areas and broadcasts their location in emergencies.

Wireless Warriors

Many U.S. soldiers are equipped with the Land Warrior system, the latest in military technology. One feature of the system is a flip-down eyepiece attached to the helmet that displays a GPS map. The map shows soldiers where their troops are and helps them communicate and get into position.

Radio microphones and over-the-ear headphones are built into their helmets too. This allows soldiers to talk to one another. The Land Warrior body armor is equipped with wireless transmitters so soldiers can signal one another in areas up to a mile (1.6 km) apart. The system also has a GPS transponder (a transmitter and receiver in one) and a computer to keep it all running. Soldiers operate the gear with a controller—shaped like a gun grip—on the chest or with buttons on the M-4 rifle.

The Land Warrior helmet (above) can also receive images from a camera on the M-4 rifle. Soldiers can use the gun to see around corners (right).

A member of the U.S. Air Force uses a handheld GPS device to check his location. Such devices help soldiers reach targets quickly.

GPS is very valuable to soldiers and commanders. They use it to navigate during night duty and to coordinate troops and supplies. Military aircraft also use GPS to find their targets. GPS can save a pilot who's been shot down. A device signals search-and-rescue missions so they can locate the crash site. The military uses GPS to conduct spy missions and search for enemy weapons. The military also uses it to detect when nuclear weapons are exploded or tested. This helps them know if other countries are developing nuclear weapons.

chapter 5

Wireless Gadgets

Wireless technology has changed more than just cell phones, PDAs, and laptops. It also has affected the ways people play and stay healthy. Sometimes existing technology is improved. Other times new technology is developed. Either way, wireless technology continues to add freedom to our lives.

Wireless Help for the Heart

Maybe you've heard of a pacemaker. Doctors can implant this device in a patient's body to monitor and adjust heart rhythms. For people who have a bad heart, a pacemaker can help them stay healthier and live longer.

Medtronic's pacemaker is only a few inches wide.

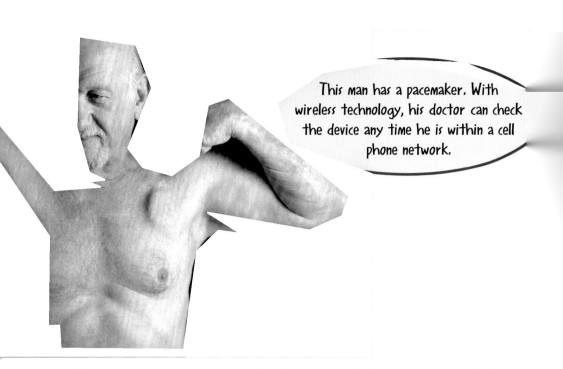

This man has a pacemaker. With wireless technology, his doctor can check the device any time he is within a cell phone network.

With older pacemakers, patients had to see their doctors regularly. Doctors would check how the pacemakers and hearts had been doing. In modern times, doctors can wirelessly monitor pacemakers to keep track of a patient's condition—without even seeing the patient.

Pacemakers continuously record and monitor the patient's heartbeat. Then they wirelessly send the information to a device similar to a cell phone. This data is sent to a service center. There it's collected and faxed to the doctor's office. The patient only needs to stay in areas with cellular service. This frees heart patients so they can maintain their regular lives.

Abiomed Inc. has developed an artificial heart that can be programmed and charged wirelessly. In the past, one of the main problems with artificial hearts was infection. The old designs had so many wires passing through the skin that bacteria could easily enter the body. The new artificial heart, called the AbioCor, eliminates that problem. It is recharged from an external battery pack. The pack transmits electrical current across the skin and into the body, where the artificial heart stores it.

Wireless technology is providing hope for people with other medical problems too. Researchers in California are developing a device to be implanted in the eye that can help people with blindness caused by certain diseases. The implant is called Argus II. It works like this: A tiny camera on the patient's eyeglasses captures an image. This image is sent wirelessly to a device the patient can wear on a belt. There, the image is converted to electrical pulses and sent back to a radio transmitter on the glasses. The transmitter then sends that signal to a receiver implanted under the eye. Finally, that receiver sends the signal through a tiny cable to a device implanted on the retina (the part of the eye that sees images). This results in a low level of vision for the patient.

What about people with profound deafness or total hearing loss? With the help of medical implants and wireless technology, the profoundly deaf can hear again. A device called the Bionic Ear has two tiny parts. One is worn behind the ear, and one is implanted in the inner ear. The part behind the ear has a microphone to receive sound. It has a wireless transmitter that sends signals over radio waves to the implant. The implant has a receiver and a microprocessor, which stimulates the hearing nerve. This creates sound in a form the ear can understand.

Hearing aids can interfere with cell phone reception, causing static on calls. This Bluetooth hearing aid solves the problem with a built-in wireless headset.

Smart Helmets

In football, forceful crashes are part of the game. Players wear lots of protective gear, so they usually walk away from these brutal hits without injuries. But sometimes hits to the head cause concussions without the players even knowing it. These serious head injuries can cause unconsciousness and memory loss.

If a player suffers more than one concussion, the brain injury could be more serious. To prevent this, scientists have developed a helmet with tiny spring-loaded buttons on the inside lining. These buttons are in continuous contact with the player's head. When the player receives a hit, the buttons wirelessly send the hit data to a laptop on the sidelines. Coaches read the laptop display. They can pull the player from the game for a medical check if the hit was too hard.

So far, these smart helmets aren't used in many football games. They are still being tested. But the information scientists are learning about head injuries will help improve prevention and treatment of injuries.

Professor Steven Broglio displays a helmet used to monitor head injuries. The helmet sends impact information to his laptop during football games.

Games and Workouts

Health and safety devices are not the only gadgets to be enhanced by wireless technology. Video games have also improved.

PlayStation and Nintendo have been making game systems for decades. In recent years, handheld games like Nintendo's Game Boy were in many kids' back pockets. But the newest handheld systems are faster, more colorful, and, best of all, wireless. With new wireless capabilities, up to sixteen players can play together on separate handheld machines without needing a hotspot. Some systems have onboard Wi-Fi so you can hop online and play with other players around the world.

Game consoles like Xbox 360, Nintendo Wii, and PlayStation 3 have many amazing features. One of the coolest is wireless controllers. These let you play without having to be tied to the game console. That can be very important when you're bouncing around in a virtual tennis or baseball game!

Visitors to an electronic gaming show try out the Wii tennis game. The Wii system uses a wireless controller.

If you're not into video games, how about a wireless device that can help your workout? Nike has hooked up with iPod to create the Nike + iPod Sport Kit. The device uses a sensor that works like a pedometer, a tool that counts or measures the steps you take. This sensor is installed in specially made shoes. The device tracks your speed, distance, and the number of calories you've burned, among other things. It sends that information wirelessly to the iPod, which displays it on the screen for you to see. The system also provides voice feedback through the iPod, including congratulating you when you reach a personal best. Of course, you also get to listen to music on the iPod while exercising.

Wireless Electricity

Wireless gadgets need power to operate. If your batteries dwindle, the device will shut off. You're back in business after the battery is charged, but that requires a cable and an outlet. However, this cable-and-plug business could soon be outdated. Recently, researchers at the Massachusetts Institute of Technology (MIT) announced a new way to power our gadgets: WiTricity.

MIT researchers stand between two wireless electricity coils. This early WiTricity system can send power across 6.5 feet (2 meters) of open space.

WiTricity is a way to transmit power without wires. When two objects resonate, or vibrate at precisely the same frequency, they create a magnetic field between them. This allows them to exchange energy. The MIT researchers developed a simple system to create this exchange. The system consists of two copper coils. One sends power, and the other receives it. In a recent test, researchers powered a 60-watt bulb using copper coils. The source coil created a magnetic field about 7 feet (2 m) in diameter and transmitted it at a frequency of 10 MHz. Seven feet away, the receiving coil was also resonating at 10 MHz. It pulled energy from the field to power the bulb.

Researchers expect WiTricity to be ready for commercial use in cell phones and other small wireless devices in three to five years.

Our world gets more wireless all the time. In the future, all our wireless devices will communicate with one another and work together perfectly. Les Williamson, the head of the technology company Cisco Australia, says systems will wirelessly anticipate our wants and needs. He imagines downloading an album of his favorite music in traffic and listening to the first half in the car. When he later enters his home, his house will recognize him. As he walks in the door, his house will wirelessly transfer the album from his car stereo to his home system and continue playing where it left off.

No one knows just how far wireless technology will advance, but one thing is sure: people love freedom. The future of wireless technology will bring more freedom than most of us can imagine.

concussion: injury to the brain caused by a blow, usually resulting in loss of consciousness

electromagnetic spectrum: a group of energy waves consisting of radio, television, radar, microwaves, infrared, visible light, ultraviolet, X-rays, gamma rays, and cosmic rays

Hertz: a unit of frequency, named for Heinrich Hertz

infrared: electromagnetic waves with a frequency range between microwaves and the visible spectrum

modulate: to change a wave pattern so that it can carry information

pedometer: a device that records footsteps for distance

piconet: a network of computing devices using Bluetooth protocols to allow one master device to interconnect with up to seven slave devices

receiver: an electronic device that receives a radio signal from an antenna and decodes the signal as sound, pictures, etc.

resonate: to pulsate or vibrate at a very precise frequency

retina: the part of the eye that sees images

stylus: a penlike device used for pointing or writing on screens

transmitter: an electronic device made up of an oscillator, modulator, and other circuits that produce radio or television wave signals

transponder: an combined transmitter and receiver that transmits a signal of its own when it receives a signal from elsewhere

Allan, Roger. "Implants Bring Hope to the Toughest Medical Handicaps." *Electronic Design* 55, no. 4 (June 29, 2007): 78.

Davis, Harold. *Absolute Beginner's Guide to Wi-Fi Wireless Networking*. Indianapolis: Que, 2004.

Fleishman, Glenn. "Is It Safe to Surf on an Open Network?" *Popular Science* 270, no. 6 (June 2007): 92.

Futuretech. "Next Generation Communication Technologies for Aerospace and Defense." *Futuretech*. October 19, 2007.

Henderson, Mark. "Wireless Power Pulls Plug on Cables." *Australian*. June 8, 2007. http://www.theaustralian.news.com.au/story/0,20867,21871209-2703,00.html (December 15, 2007).

Hopkins, Jim. "Sports Gear Gets More Gadgety." *USA Today*, October 22, 2007.

Johnson, Joel. "Face Dialing." *Popular Mechanics* 184, no 9 (September 2007): 122.

LaGesse, David. "Five Fresh Uses for GPS." *U.S. News & World Report*, August 14, 2007.

Lewis, Barry D., and Peter T. Davis. *Wireless Networks for Dummies*. Hoboken, NJ: Wiley, 2004.

McCarthy, Erin. "WiTricity." Popular *Mechanics* 184, no. 9 (September 2007): 20.

Ninemsn. "Gadgets of Future to Be 'Tied Together.'" *Ninemsn*. September 24, 2007. http://news.ninemsn.com.au/article.aspx?id=254917 (December 15, 2007).

Schactman, Noah. "The Wireless Warrior." *Popular Mechanics* 184, no. 5 (May 2007): 70.

Tucker, Patrick. "Privacy and Wireless Devices." *Futurist* 41, no. 3 (May–June 2007): 12.

Victoria, Shannon. "U.N. Agency Gives Boost to WiMax." *New York Times*, October 20, 2007, C8.

Ask Dr. Universe

http://www.wsu.edu/DrUniverse/Contents.html

At this website, sponsored by Washington State University, kids can get answers to science questions such as "How many stars and galaxies are in the Universe?" Find out everything from how Bluetooth works to what causes hiccups.

Dragonfly TV Science Fair/PBS Kids Go!

http://pbskids.org/dragonflytv/scifair/index.html

Go to this website to turn the investigations you see on *Dragonfly TV* into your own science projects. Besides projects, the site has games, a message board, and you can even watch the show. Type "wireless" into the search window to find cool wireless stories or experiments.

Fridell, Ron. *Military Technology*. Cool Science series. Minneapolis: Lerner Publishing Company, 2007. Technology has changed everything, including the way countries go to war. Readers will learn the surprising ways technology can make all the difference on the battlefield.

Greatest Engineering Achievements of the Twentieth Century

http://www.greatachievements.org

This site, sponsored by the National Academy of Engineering, links to pages that explain advances in technology in ways that kids would understand and enjoy. Many wireless topics are discussed, and it includes timelines.

Koelhoffer, Tara. *Computers and Technology*. New York: Chelsea House, 2006. This book explores recent advances in technology, from computers to handheld devices, and how they affect our everyday lives.

Science News for Kids

http:// www.sciencenewsforkids.com

This website provides cool science news for kids ages nine to fourteen. Type "wireless" in the search window to find the latest in wireless news.

Woodford, Chris, Ben Morgan, and Clint Witchalls. *How Cool Stuff Works*. London: DK Publishing, 2005. Colorfully illustrated, this book captures young readers as it explores and explains modern technology including X-rays, the Internet, space-age materials, fluorescent lights, and Velcro.

Minnesota author Mary Firestone has written over thirty books of nonfiction for children. She lives in Saint Paul with her son Adam and their Coonhound, Mimi.